So You're Expecting to be a Grandparent!

S0-AGC-121

More than 50 Things You Should Know about Grandparenting
(so you don't drive your kid crazy!)

By Mary Ellen Pinkham and Dale Ronda Burg

Scratch inside cover when scent fades.

© 2006 Mary Ellen Pinkham and Dale Ronda Burg

ALL RIGHTS RESERVED

No part of this publication may be reproduced or transmitted in any form or by any means, electronic or mechanical, including photocopy, recording, or any other information storage and retrieval systems, without the written permission of the publisher. For information, address Pinkham Publishing, P.O. Box 390221, Edina, MN 55439 or visit www.maryellenproducts.com

Pinkham Publishing makes every effort to use acid-free and recycled paper.

PRINTED IN THE UNITED STATES OF AMERICA

First printing: July 2006

ISBN 13: 978-0-941298-43-8; ISBN 10: 0-941298-43-4

To great expectations for our friends who are—or will be—grandparents.
(Of COURSE you don't look old enough!)

INTRODUCTION

So you're going to be a grandparent! First come the ahhs and then the uh-ohs. A grandchild! *Can they afford this baby?* Will it be a boy or a girl! I hope it's healthy! I've been waiting for this! *Do they know what they're in for?*

Do you know what *you're* in for? The next few months are going to be exciting, emotional, and surprising. This book is meant to help you know what to expect.

The most important thing for you to do is to stand back a little. Your child is an adult now. Try to recall his or her reaction to your unsolicited advice in the past, and (just as you yourself have counseled), learn from experience.

Offer congratulations and support. Try not to give suggestions until—and unless—you're asked. And stay focused on the positive: the darling grandchild who will be yours very soon!

(But if all else fails: Lie down, open this book, lay it over your face, and take a little break while you breathe in the relaxing scent of lavender.)

MY BABY'S EXPECTING!

You and your child will probably draw closer than ever as you anticipate the great event. But you're in for a few surprises along the way.

Perfect love sometimes does not come until the first grandchild.

—Welsh Proverb

Get an okay before you spread the news

You're bursting to tell, but don't begin working the phone lines, posting stuff on your website, and investigating the cost of skywriting until the expectant parents give you the go-ahead. They may want to deliver the news personally to others. Also, they may want to keep the news under wraps until they pass a particular pregnancy milestone or consider how the news will impact their jobs.

You may not get to choose what you'll be called

One of our friends loved his grandson, but hated it when the tyke hurled himself forward shouting "Grandpa!" in public— perhaps because Gramps' date was a thirty-five-year-old.

You may or may not want to be called Grandma or Grandpa. Maybe it's an age thing. Or maybe you simply want to distinguish yourself from the other grandparents. Pick a word from your family's native language, or make one up. (One neighborhood grandfather calls himself "R.P.," for Revered Patriarch.)

But be prepared for the possibility that your kids will have their own strong preference for what you should be called. And perhaps you'll all be overruled. Your grandchild may come up with a special name for you.

*J*ust about the time a woman thinks
her work is done, she becomes
a grandmother.

—Edward H. Dreschnack

5

When a child is born, so are grandmothers.

—Judith Levy

The kids may not want the heirloom furniture

It may not meet current safety standards. The slats on the crib may be spaced too far apart; the paint may be lead-based. Of course it's also possible they simply prefer their taste to yours.

They might name the baby after one of the in-laws

Or they may pick a name that sounds to you like something on a map, in a car showroom, or on an astronomy chart. If you can't say something nice, just say something ambiguous, such as "That's a name, all right."

Remember, names come in cycles. What sounds odd to your ears now may become the Jennifer or Michael of tomorrow. Or not. Maybe the child will become an entertainment star.

*I'm going to be your grandpa!
I have the biggest smile.
I've been waiting to meet you
For such a long, long while.*

—Billy Crystal

It's amazing how grandparents seem so young once you become one.

—Author Unknown

You'll probably want to kick your bad habits

Give up smoking (if you haven't already). Otherwise, they'll never let you baby-sit. This is also a good time to make those other resolutions (diet, exercise) so you'll be in better shape to lend a pair of hands. Of course, the biggest help is your loving concern. (Though money is also welcome.)

A grandmother is a mother who has a second chance.

—Author Unknown

The mom-to-be probably won't think what you're buying is as cute as you do

You do tend to look a gift horse in the mouth if what you really wanted was a collie dog. There's nothing worse than getting a gift you hate from someone whose feelings you don't want to hurt and who also expects to see it on display. To avoid problems, shop together and let her pick. Or give cash. What's more important: the gift (you liked the lamp with the clowns, she liked the one with the ducks) or your child's happiness?

You'd better learn how to use the Internet

Most young parents are used to communicating electronically. If you want to get updates and the cute-baby pictures on a regular basis (and if you want to pass them along to others) you had better get busy learning how to send email and send snapshots online.

*S*ince pregnancy, my breasts, rear end,
and even my feet have grown.
The only thing that hasn't gotten
bigger is my bladder.

—Author Unknown

It won't all come back to you

And if it does, some of it will be wrong, anyway. There are newer, better ways to keep babies safe and happy. Read about how pregnancy is managed today and new birthing practices. Tour the maternity facility, and get up-to-date information about equipment and terminology. Find out if you can take a course for expectant grandparents at the local hospital. That will reassure parents you're well equipped for babysitting. (It'll reassure you, too.)

Grandparents hold our tiny hands just a little while, but our hearts forever.

—Author Unknown

*N*ever have children,
only grandchildren.

—Gore Vidal

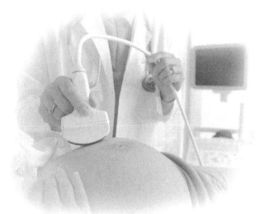

The doctor's advice will trump yours

The doctor has been through more births than you, so don't try to compete. Just be sure you seem informed and up-to-date—for example, when you come along for an ultrasound, you should know you're supposed to listen for a whoosh and not a thump. Earn your credibility.

You'll have a great opportunity to bond with your daughter and daughter-in-law

Pregnant women are usually very interested in talking about the amazing things that are happening to them, and you'll probably be a better listener than dad. Read whatever pregnancy book she's reading; you'll have more to talk about.

You may not always agree with some of your children's plans

The baby belongs to your child, not to you. Your child is the adult in charge, and your job is to support your child. Because he/she is the parent, that's why. Besides, a child who is not in a power struggle with you is more likely to hear what you're saying.

*Grandmother-grandchild relationships
are simple. Grandmas are short on
criticism and long on love.*

—Author Unknown

You'll have sentimental impulses

You may find yourself interested in making a family tree, preparing an oral history, or putting together a scrapbook. Perhaps you'll knit a blanket for the baby. If you ask the parents to choose the colors, they may actually enjoy using the blanket.

Your behavior may be misinterpreted

If you're expressing concern, you may be accused of butting in; if you're trying to give them space, they may think you're not interested. Parents-to-be want the grandparents to share in their excitement, so say how much you are looking forward to the grandchild. They also want reassurance; so say how certain you are that they will be good parents.

It's funny what happens when you become a grandparent. You start to act all goofy and do things you never thought you'd do.

—Mike Krzyzewski

Grandchildren: The only people who can get more out of you than the IRS.

—Gene Perret

You will never run out of things to worry about

If you think there's a situation that's a cause for very serious concern, consult an expert and ask him or her how best to deal with it. Otherwise, try to keep a lid on your worries. Your anxiety will just ramp up theirs.

THE WAITING GAME

Waiting for your own baby to arrive was a piece of cake compared to waiting for your baby's baby to arrive. Just try to remember that women's bodies are remarkably effective at producing healthy children even under the most adverse circumstances. So chances are that most of your concerns can be put to rest.

Vegans and vegetarians can have perfectly healthy children

While many vegans are slim—and might need to add a few more pounds than the average-sized person during pregnancy—their diet needn't stand in the way of having a healthy baby. You can meet all the calcium, folic acid and other requirements necessary for a good pregnancy on a vegetarian and even a vegan diet.

Didn't we, like our grandchildren, begin with a childhood we thought would never end? Now, all of a sudden, I'm older than my parents were when I thought they were old.

—Lois Wyse

Gaining as little as four pounds is normal during the first trimester

The March of Dimes recommends a 25- to 35-pound gain for most people. If you're a little underweight when you become pregnant, they suggest you gain 28 to 40 pounds, and if you're a little overweight at first, the guidelines are 15 to 25 pounds. But these are only general guidelines.

Gaining too little may in fact put the mom-to-be at risk of having a too-small (under five pounds) baby. But during the first trimester women may gain very little and may even lose weight since they often lose their appetite and their stomach is unsettled. If the pregnant mom is eating healthy foods, looks healthy and feels healthy, and the baby is growing, everything is likely to be fine.

Packing on the pounds between the 15th and 20th weeks is also normal

Five to ten pounds is typical at this point in the pregnancy. If the mom-to-be doesn't have time to buy or prepare healthful meals or snacks, you could volunteer to do it. But *only* if you're sure the mom won't feel criticized.

You must remember that when you're pregnant, you're eating for two. But you must also remember that one of you is the size of a golf ball. Let's not go overboard with it.

—Dave Barry

Exercising is fine

Thirty minutes of exercise a day is recommended. It makes a pregnant woman feel good, build strength for labor, and avoid some common physical problems in pregnancy. Walking, dancing, swimming, biking, aerobics, or yoga are ideal. Women who are used to more challenging exercise can probably continue, if the doctor okays it. But after the third month, a pregnant woman should avoid exercises that involve lying flat on her back.

Pregnant women can fly

If there are no obstetric or medical concerns, a pregnant woman is welcome to fly up to the 36th week, or the 35th week for international flights. Wearing support stockings and moving about to prevent blood clots are recommended.

Grandchildren are the dots that connect lines from generation to generation.

—Gail Lumet Buckley

If nothing is going well, call
your grandmother.

—Italian Proverb

"Stress" is not always what it seems

What some people might consider stress, other people consider a job perk, or there would be no prosecuting attorneys or Olympic snowboarders. It's cause for concern if a pregnant woman is chronically anxious, depressed, or unable to sleep. If she is following her normal routine without adverse effects, it's not.

She might be very moody

Pregnant women are sometimes unpredictable. Of course non-pregnant women are sometimes unpredictable.

Life is tough enough without having someone kick you from the inside.

—Rita Rudner

Dad might be hormonal, too

At least one study has found hormonal changes in men before and right after the birth of a child. A common symptom of these changes is depression, and the remedies are the common-sense ones: get more sleep, exercise, and eat properly.

We should all have one person who knows how to bless us despite the evidence. Grandmother was that person to me.

—Phyllis Theroux

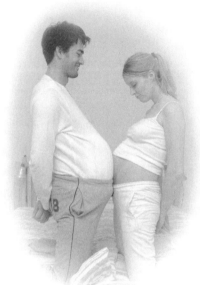

*The most common pregnancy craving
is for men to be the ones
who get pregnant.*

—Author Unknown

He also may start packing on the pounds

More than half of all spouses may share some of the symptoms of pregnancy, including nausea, headache, backache, and most commonly, weight gain, usually at the end of the first trimester and again at delivery. The French even have a word for it: *couvade*.

Two species of male monkeys tend to do the same. Scientists say a chemical emitted by their pregnant mates causes hormonal changes that make marmosets and cotton-top tamarins gain weight. These monkeys are very involved dads, and the scientists speculate they bulk up to give them energy to carry the babies around. So the weight gain could indicate that he'll be a good father.

*Grandparents are God's gift
to children.*

—Bill Cosby

You might want to start building the baby's nest egg

You can make a yearly gift of up to $11,000 tax free, but you're also going to want to think about college funding. Section 529 plans let you put aside money tax free to prepay tuition, and Coverdell Accounts allow you to put away $2000 a year tax free, but the assets belong to the child at age 18. Could be a problem when said 18-year-old decides to fund a motorcycle or a tattoo.

Yes, she IS going to wear that

After actress Demi Moore posed naked (but with body paint) on
the cover of *Vanity Fair*, the "bump" went public. Maternity
bikinis don't raise an eyebrow.

*H*ave children while your parents are
still young enough to take care
of them.

—Rita Rudner

You won't want to make plans around the due date

Don't schedule any trips or major events on either side of the due date. Babies don't necessarily come when they're expected, and you won't rest easy until the baby's safely here and the jitters of the first few days are over.

I wish the stork did bring babies.

—Dale Burg

LABOR AND DELIVERY

Many things have changed since you had your baby. The hospital experience can be a family affair, where the attendees may also include siblings, grandparents, and others; the same room may be used for labor and delivery; the medical people may use different equipment; and even the customary position for laboring may not be the one you remember. But the excitement and joy are the same.

She might want to use a midwife

Expectant mothers may choose to give birth in a hospital, in a freestanding birth center (that is generally staffed by midwifes and birth attendants), or at home. And there are pros and cons for each choice. State your point of view (once); then recognize it's her right to make the decision. If you get some more information about the various options, you may find you're less anxious about her choice. See the Resources section.

You may confuse the labor room with a hotel room

At many hospitals today, the expectant mom remains in a single room—the LDRP (Labor/Delivery/Recovery/Postpartum Room)—from beginning to end. And except for the fact that you check out with one more person than when you came in, it might be mistaken for an elegant guestroom. The "birthing suite," as it may be called, may contain a sofa sleeper, a partner bed, a Jacuzzi, a stereo with CD players, Internet access, a plasma TV, a patio, or a garden—or all of the above.

Grandchildren are God's way of compensating us for growing old.

—Mary H. Waldrip

*Becoming a grandmother:
There is no fun for
old people like it!*

—Hannah Whitall Smith

They may want you in the delivery room

Though many people are enthusiastic at the prospect of witnessing the baby's birth, others may have mixed feelings. They're concerned about being upset, flustered, embarrassed, or all of the above. But those who've been through it report that it goes so fast—and it's all so exciting—that you needn't be concerned. You'll have to take their word for it until you find out for yourself.

They may want everyone in the delivery room

More than ever, pregnancy is a shared experience. While it used to be primarily a mother-daughter thing, now the dads are deeply involved along with the grandparents, siblings, friends, kids from a previous marriage—everybody except the pizza delivery man.

*Surely, these are two of the most
satisfying experiences in life:
being a grandchild or
a grandparent.*

—Donald A. Norberg

They may want no one in the delivery room

The expectant mom may prefer not to be the star of her own reality show when she gives birth. If she wants to keep the moment private, defer to her wishes. Everyone will have lots of time to get to know the baby. Besides, this is her last chance to exercise total control. Once the baby arrives, it's over.

I have a warm feeling after playing with my grandchildren. It's the liniment working.

—Author Unknown

There's plenty for you to do

You can offer a lot of help—both to distract and to comfort the mom while she's in labor. Offer in advance to take responsibility for bringing along a deck of cards, CDs, DVDs and the players, the camera, backup batteries, and so forth. Volunteer to be the photographer or the assistant. You're the one who can brush mom's hair, rub her back, fetch a drink, find some slippers, and make any necessary phone calls.

An IV is no cause for panic

The doctor may have told the mom-to-be to expect to be on an IV, but no one may have thought to tell you. If a woman doesn't eat or drink during labor—either by choice or under doctor's orders—she may become dehydrated or weak, and an IV can deliver fluid and nutrition. It's also an effective way to deliver any medicine that might be needed.

*H*olding grandbabies in my arms
makes me realize the miracle
my husband and I started.

—Betty Ford

They might not be monitoring the baby all along

Though the use of the monitor has been on the rise, there have been many false-positive readings that increased the likelihood of cesareans and other procedures. So in 2005, the American College of Gynecologists and Obstetricians recommended that heart rates for patients without complications be reviewed just every 30 minutes during the first stage of labor and 15 minutes during the second.

If pregnancy were a book they would cut the last two chapters.

—Nora Ephron

The pregnant mom may be upright for delivery

To have a woman in stirrups and on her back for delivery was very helpful for doctors, who could observe all the goings-on very comfortably, but it wasn't so great for the moms. Since they were pushing against gravity, an episiotomy was probably more inevitable.

Nowadays, many women labor in "birthing beds," chair-like devices with adjustable handles and foot rests. The birthing beds come apart during the pushing stage so the laboring mom can get into the upright sitting position that is common for delivery today. She may be encouraged to experiment with positions common in other cultures that she may find comfortable: squatting, kneeling, standing or leaning forward during delivery.

They may save the umbilical cord

Hospitals used to discard umbilical cord blood. But researchers discovered that it helps in the treatment of certain cancers and other diseases. Since it can be salvaged without harm to mother or baby, women today often bank their cords for future use in the event of family illness or transplant situations, despite the high storage costs for this self-created medical insurance.
See the Resource Section.

WELCOME, STRANGER!

Real newborns, of course, don't look like the rosy pink, scrubbed and groomed babies you see in the delivery room in the movies. A real baby will be slightly the worse for wear, like any weary traveler after a hard journey. But naturally, to all of you, the baby will be beautiful.

The new parents may be concerned about baby's appearance

After a few hours squeezing through a tight birth canal the baby's head may look stretched out or even pointed. Fluid squeezed into the scalp and friction between the baby's head and mom's pelvic bones may cause lumps on the scalp. The baby will be curled up after nine months in tight quarters, and baby's genitals will be swollen because of extra hormones released just before birth. Baby's skin may be downy, rashy, or spotted, too. Reassure the new mom and dad that all those problems will clear up.

Holding a grandchild who is only a few minutes old is a truly wonderful thing.

—Rita Seidelman

The color of the baby's skin, hair, and eyes may be a surprise

Newborn babies of all races and ethnicities have thin, dark red
to purple skin, caused by the red blood vessels under the surface.
Though most babies are bald, when they're born with hair it's
most often (but not always) dark and not necessarily like the
mother's. Brunettes can be born to blondes and redheads to
brunettes. Usually a newborn's hair falls out within a month, and
the color and texture of the new hair may be totally different.
While most Caucasian babies have dark grey-blue eyes, other
babies have dark grey-brown eyes. Eye color may change within a
few weeks. At six months babies' eyes are usually the color they'll
remain for a lifetime.

Grandparents are similar to a piece of string: handy to have and easily wrapped around the fingers of their grandchildren.

—Author Unknown

The in-laws may claim the baby resembles their side of the family

If they are taking the credit for the little tyke's beauty, let them delude themselves. You can remain on amicable terms while having the satisfaction of knowing those good looks are thanks to your family's genes.

The baby may in fact resemble the in-law's side of the family

There is a theory that newborns look like the father to encourage him to bond with the child, but that may or may not appear to be the case with your baby. The truth is that you won't really know what the baby looks like for a while. Babies' appearances can change remarkably during the first few months.

•

You may be asked to leave right after the baby is born

A newborn usually remains awake for about an hour after the birth, then naps for four to six hours. Many hospitals encourage mother, baby, and father to spend the post-delivery hour—which has come to be known as "the golden hour"—alone together. (One reason is that when mothers start breastfeeding immediately, the process tends to go more smoothly.)

Then, while baby sleeps, friends and relatives may gather to celebrate.

Breast feeding: The milk is always the right temperature and it comes in an attractive container.

—Irena Chalmers

Grandparents sprinkle stardust over the lives of little children.

—Alex Haley

You'll want to preserve your memories of the day

To create a special keepsake, record the news broadcasts and put aside a daily newspaper and current magazine. You can do the same thing annually or at five-year intervals. It's an inexpensive and interesting tradition for the child to keep up. Won't he or she be surprised, a couple of decades down the road, to see how weird the fashions were and how inexpensive everything was "way back then"?

BRINGING BABY HOME

The first few days of new parenthood (and grandparenthood) are exhilarating—and exhausting.

Baby will need a car seat to ride home from the hospital

Grandparents are sometimes more casual about car seats than parents, who rightly insist that infants never ride without one. The seat should be rear-facing, and (if the car has air bags) be installed in the rear of the car. If you're going to look for a car seat in a thrift shop or at a tag sale, make sure it meets current crash test standards. See the Resource Section.

The new parents may be awkward with their baby

If you can't think back all the way to how you were with your own first baby, then just think back to how you were when you were dealing with your first cell phone. It takes a while to master all new techniques, including diapering or bathing a baby. If you share this insight with your kids, they'll probably be grateful.

When grandparents enter the door, discipline flies out the window.

—Ogden Nash

Your kids may micromanage your handling of the baby

They'll tell you exactly how the baby should be bathed, washed, and fed, based on what they've learned at the hospital or from a book. It's possible they have something new to teach you—and it's equally possible they're just being anxious. Just go along. You want to build their confidence so they will eventually leave you unobserved and you can spoil the baby to your heart's content.

Your suggestions may not be welcome

Unless you see them doing something that's absolutely dangerous to the new baby, resist commenting. Focus your energies on your child rather than theirs. You can probably offer many things that would be more appreciated than your opinion. Have a dinner sent in, offer to pay for a house call by a masseuse or hairdresser, bring mom something comfy but fresh to replace that tired maternity robe, or just offer to run an errand or babysit for an hour or two. (Even a breastfeeding mom can take a short break.)

The reason grandchildren and grandparents get along so well is that they have a common enemy.

—Sam Levenson

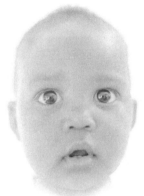

*N*o cowboy was ever faster on the
draw than a grandparent pulling
a baby picture out of a wallet.

—Author Unknown

You will not believe the amount of equipment one little baby requires

We all know you managed without an electric wipe warmer (or even prepackaged wipes). Please don't tell us again how you had to rub the sticks together to build the fire to warm the bottle. Going on about it will just irritate your child. Instead, spend your energy figuring out how to work the newfangled stuff you're likely to use. At least practice collapsing the stroller when the baby is not in it.

The parents will need some time alone with the baby

Even though they are happy to have everyone make a fuss about the new baby, it is also important for them to learn to be a family. Though the pull of the new grandchild is tremendous, try to resist and to give them some space.

Our grandchildren accept us for ourselves, without rebuke or effort to change us, as no one in our entire lives has ever done, not our parents, siblings, spouses, friends—and hardly ever our own grown children.

—Ruth Goode

You may not agree with the mother's decision regarding breastfeeding

In 2005, the American Academy of Pediatrics recommended exclusive breastfeeding for approximately six months and supported breastfeeding for a year and beyond, as long as mutually desired by the mother and child. But they're her breasts and it's her choice. Plenty of babies have thrived on either regime, and your opinion will not be appreciated unless it is asked for. And possibly not even then.

It will be very provocative to suggest formula if the mother is breastfeeding

Well-meaning grandmothers are sometimes concerned that the baby isn't getting enough milk. The doctor will keep a watchful eye on baby's weight during post-partum visits. And of course you can't check a breast-feeding baby's input. But you can check outgo. The rule of thumb is six to eight wet diapers a day and two to five bowel movements for a newborn. You can't always tell whether a disposable is dry or not—the manufacturers add a chemical that crystallizes when urine hits it—so if you're using this method, line it with a tissue.

*There's no place like home,
except Grandma's.*

—Author Unknown

Tub baths are recommended for new moms

Once upon a time, mothers didn't bathe until a month after giving birth. Today bathing is recommended to soothe and clean the genital area. But the doctor has to give the go-ahead. If you want to help, make sure the tub is very clean and offer to draw the bath.

Exercising is encouraged

Old wisdom: Just keeping busy gets you back in shape.

New wisdom: Not only will the right exercise tone up stretched muscles, keep your back strong, and prevent other physical problems, but by releasing endorphins, it can pump you up. The American College of Obstetrics and Gynecology says that after an uncomplicated delivery, there are no known complications caused by a return to training and not even when you jump back in—though they do recommend a gradual process.

They say genes skip generations.
Maybe that's why grandparents find
their grandchildren so likeable.

—Joan McIntosh

I let my grandchildren eat junk food and watch violent cartoons. Then they love me.

—Gail Parent

You'll want to equip your house for a baby

Your kids will find it easier to visit if you have your own crib and baby supplies. They'll also appreciate your babyproofing in advance of a young visitor. Get down on your hands and knees to get the baby's perspective on everything and figure out how to secure whatever might tempt the baby to grab, suck on, or poke a finger into.

"Back is best" for babies in cribs

To avoid Sudden Infant Death Syndrome (SIDS), and unless the doctor directs otherwise for medical reasons, never place a baby to sleep on his or her stomach until he/she is able to turn over alone. Remove any heavy, fluffy pillows, blankets, or bedding such as down, sheepskin, or featherbedding; don't hang anything above the crib with ribbons or strings longer than seven inches; and don't put anything in the crib that can fall on or bump against the baby—hence, no toys.

The slats should be spaced no farther apart than 2 3/8" to prevent head entrapment, and if a blanket must be used, it should be placed no higher than a baby's chest and be tucked in under the crib mattress.

The parents may sleep with the baby

About 70 percent of parents do it, and some experts say it's okay if precautions are observed: Make sure there is no bedding that could smother the baby and that baby can't roll off the bed or be caught between the mattress and headboard or wall.

Large persons, persons who have been drinking or drugging or who are very sound sleepers, and pets shouldn't sleep with the baby.

Finally, the infant should be placed between his mother and the wall because only a mother's instinctual awareness of a baby's location is totally trustworthy. See the Resource Section.

The baby is probably warm enough

Babies getting used to life outside the womb often need some time to reset their temperature gauge, but a baby who is calm and sleeping and eating well is probably comfortable. Check also that the hands, feet, and head are neither too warm nor too cool.

There's no need to pile on the sweaters and blankets (particularly since the latter can increase the risk of SIDS). One more layer than adults would wear is sufficient protection.

You and the parents may disagree about vaccinations

In the past thirty years, the list of routine vaccinations has come to include Hepatitis B, diphtheria, tetanus, pertussis, haemophilus Influenza type B, inactivated poliovirus, measles, mumps and rubella, varicella, pneumococcal, influenza, and Hepatitis A, but there is some controversy about which vaccinations to give. Check the Resources section of this book. But you get the last word on one, since it applies to you. Federal guidelines call for adults to be vaccinated against pertussis (also known as whooping cough), with a booster every five to ten years. Outbreaks are on the rise, and while the disease isn't life-threatening to adults, it can be fatal to children who haven't received all their shots.

The simplest toy, one which even the youngest child can operate, is called a grandparent.

—Sam Levenson

Your children may put the baby on a schedule

You may have thought that idea went out the window a long time ago. But current thinking is that establishing a daytime and bedtime schedule with consistent, enjoyable routines helps both the physical and mental development of the child. The feeding schedule may be a little more flexible.

Few things are more delightful than grandchildren fighting over your lap.

—Doug Larson

Even an experienced professional may be overwhelmed by a new baby

If she's used to being in control, she may be unaccustomed to or uncomfortable about asking for help. Take the initiative and offer some, on a regular basis. You can wash clothes, do the dishes, clean up, walk the pet, run errands (or hire someone to help!) Bringing over some special dishes or a little gift for dad is a nice idea, too; sometimes his needs are minimized when the focus is on baby and mom.

No matter how independent she is, a new mom may want some coddling

The offer of a home-cooked (or good store-bought) meal may be especially welcome during the first few weeks of motherhood. The drop-off gives you a good excuse for a short visit.

The baby's crying may stress out everyone

Even when the doctor has determined that the baby's crying isn't due to any problem such as food sensitivities, and after you've tried all the logical remedies (feeding, changing, etc.), the baby may cry more than you expect. If it's been a while since you've been around a baby, or if you're inexperienced, it may be unsettling. But bear in mind that it comes to an end. The crying usually peaks at about six weeks, and infants tend to settle down—almost magically, people say—once they're three months old.

118

Grandma always made you feel she had been waiting to see just you all day, and now the day was complete.

—Marcy DeMaree

Your children may seem anxious about leaving you alone with the baby

It will help if they believe you're up to date on the latest advice—you've taken a course for expectant grandparents at the local hospital or read any book on baby care that they have recommended.

A grandmother is a babysitter who watches the kids instead of the television.

—Author Unknown

A mother becomes a true grandmother the day she stops noticing the terrible things her children do because she is so enchanted with the wonderful things her grandchildren do.

—Lois Wyse

You may be too anxious to be alone with the baby

Say so, and volunteer your help in other ways. Remember that for new parents, losing all your freedom is a huge adjustment. Simple things like taking a shower, catching some sleep or running to the store are now dictated by baby's schedule. So offer a few hours here or there for mom to go off-duty and take care of personal or household errands.

You may want to limit your babysitting duty

If you feel you're being taken for granted or imposed upon, or you aren't up to babysitting as much as your child would like, it's okay to say so. And do it sooner rather than later, so you can express yourself calmly. Explain that you love the baby but you have other commitments and obligations that mean setting limits on the babysitting time.

The best babysitters, of course, are the baby's grandparents. You feel completely comfortable entrusting your baby to them for long periods of time, which is why many grandparents flee to Florida.

—Dave Barry

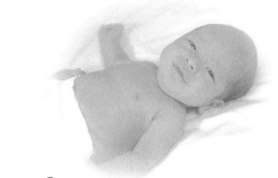

A child needs a grandparent to grow a little more securely into an unfamiliar world.

—Charles and Ann Morse

The new parents may seem hypersensitive

Be patient. The mother is dealing with her hormones. The father is dealing with her hormones. They're nervous and overtired, overwhelmed and frightened by this new responsibility. Faced with dealing with a newborn—its incessant needs, yucky moments, incomprehensible crying spells—they may even be having second thoughts about whether they're cut out for parenthood. Once the baby starts smiling, everyone will calm down.

The new mom may have an attack of baby blues

Be sympathetic. Reassure her that no one's perfect. Do what you can to lift her spirits: bring over a funny DVD, treat the couple to dinner out, send over a hairdresser or a masseuse. Get her out of the house if possible, or give her time alone if she wants some. (Unlike other depression, baby blues don't get worse if one spends time alone.) The blues should pass in a couple of weeks. (But if they don't, encourage mom to see a doctor. Postpartum depression, or PPD, is not the same as baby blues and may require medical intervention.)

Everyone needs to have access both to grandparents and grandchildren in order to be a full human being.

—Margaret Mead

Being a houseguest right after the birth may not be a good idea

Make the offer to come in if you live out of town, but give the new parents an out. They simply may not be able to deal with a new presence other than the baby's—no matter how considerate and helpful you might be. Maybe now's the time for you to go on a little vacation, rest, and plan a visit down the road a bit, when the parents have gotten into some kind of routine and recovered their composure. Bonus: a slightly older baby will be slightly more responsive.

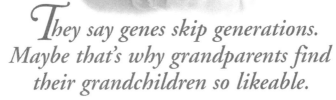

*They say genes skip generations.
Maybe that's why grandparents find
their grandchildren so likeable.*

—Joan McIntosh

You may regret living far away

Use the Internet to search out airline deals for making trips, but if traveling is a problem, equip your home with a crib and other necessary items and send tickets for them to come to you. Emailing notes and photos helps keep everyone in touch.

An extra-special touch: Go to Build-A-Bear and make a recorded message on the voice box that goes inside the stuffed toy so your voice will be familiar.

What you may not expect

How thrilling it will be to have a grandchild. Enjoy every moment of it.

Resources:

There are many useful resources on the web. These are some that we have found to be helpful on various topics.

Car seats, other subjects: American Academy of Pediatrics, aap.org

Childproofing: Consumer Product Safety Commission, cpsc.gov

Cord blood: parentsguidetocordblood.com

Co-sleeping: attachmentparenting.org, naturalchild.com, askdrsears.com, kidshealth.com

Financial advice: savingsforcollege.com

General grandparenting: American Association of Retired Persons, aarp.com (type *grandparenting* for links), grandparenting.org, grandparentstoday.com

Midwives: choicemidwives.org, askyourmidwife.com

Nutrition: U.S. Food and Drug Administration, cfsan.fda.gov (Click on *Food Safety for Moms-to-Be* and on *Women's Health*)

Pregnancy and labor: American College of Obstetrics and Gynecology, acog.org and March of Dimes, marchofdimes.com

Vaccination and other topics: Center for Disease Control and Prevention, cdc.gov

Thanks for ideas to Jennifer Burgess, Connie Carlson, Donna Hanzal, Laura Lander, Linda Lock, Susan S. Meadors, Laurie Neador, and Norman Seidelman.

The Perfect Gift for New Moms...

For Crying Out Loud!
Over 50 Ways to Help Your Baby Stop Crying (So You Don't Start)
By Mary Ellen Pinkham

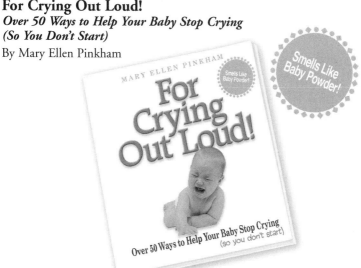

This book is destined to appear at every baby shower. It's a must-have for all new and expecting mothers. Over 50 surprising, creative, effective, mom-tested ways to help keep a baby happy and tear-free. Sprinkled with inspirational quotes from famous people and charming baby pictures.

Only $9.95 per book and $2.00 per book for shipping and handling.
Mail check or money order to:
Mary Ellen Products, P.O. Box 390221, Edina, MN 55439-0221

BYE-BYE BABY STAINS

"After the miracle of childbirth comes the miracle of laundry."

How does one little baby generate such a mess? So many moms asked me for a way to remove formula, spit-ups and other baby stains that we decided there was a need for this one-of-a-kind product. Squirt it on and watch the most impossible stains disappear. Even old stains from hand-me-downs will be "all gone."

Two formulas: Formula 1 for whites and colorfast items, and Formula 2 for colored clothing. Each 8 oz. bottle is only $5.99, plus $2.00 per bottle for shipping and handling.

Mail check or money order to:

Mary Ellen Products, P.O. Box 390221, Edina, MN 55439-0221

or go to www.maryellenproducts.com

LOOKING FOR MORE GREAT GIFT BOOKS?

Check out our website. We offer discount prices and we'll even pay for the mailing or shipping.